Us...

Garden Flowers

Barry Ambrose

Consultant: James Armitage, from The Royal
Horticultural Society Garden, Wisley, England

Illustrated by William Giles and Ian Jackson

Usborne Quicklinks

The Usborne Quicklinks Website is packed with thousands of links to all the best websites on the internet. The websites include information, video clips, sounds, games and animations that support and enhance the information in Usborne internet-linked books.

To visit the recommended websites for Spotter's Garden Flowers, go to the Usborne Quicklinks Website at **www.usborne-quicklinks.com** and enter the keywords: **spotters garden flowers**

Internet safety

When using the internet please follow the internet safety guidelines displayed on the Usborne Quicklinks Website. The recommended websites in Usborne Quicklinks are regularly reviewed and updated, but Usborne Publishing Ltd is not responsible for the content or availability of any website other than its own. We recommend that children are supervised while using the internet.

Contents

How to use this book

There are hundreds of different flowers to spot in gardens and parks around Britain and Europe. This book shows you some of them and helps you identify them.

Identification

Each different kind of flower is called a species. The description next to the picture of each species tells you what details to look for, where you are likely to find it and how big it might be.

Name and description of species

➡ Japanese rose

Lots of small, thin prickles on branches. Wrinkled leaves. Single, scented flowers. Round, orange-red fruit appears in autumn. 2m tall. Summer-autumn.

The season when the plant usually flowers in Britain

Average height from the ground to the top of the flower

Colours

To make it easy for you to look them up, the flowers in this book are arranged by their most common colour. Although the picture shows the flower as one colour, when you go out spotting, you may see the same flower in a different colour.

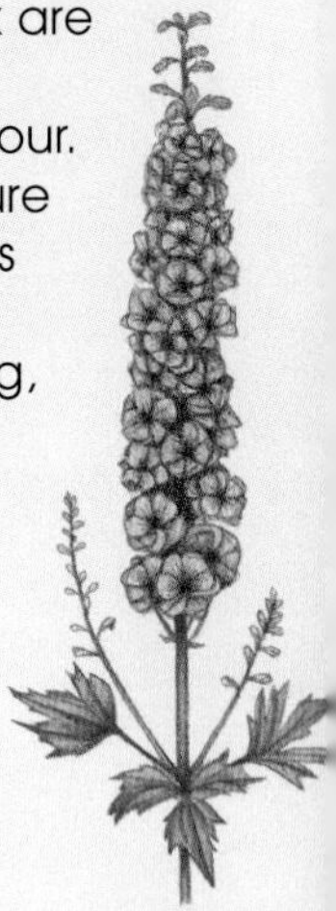

Delphiniums are in the blue section of this book, but they can also be mauve or white.

Picture of fruit to help you identify the plant in a different season

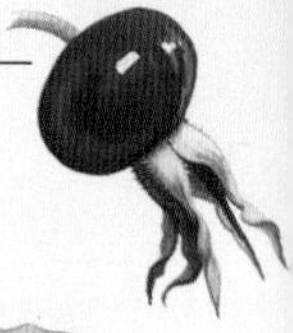

Picture of species (not drawn to scale)

4

What grows where?

The flowers in this book can be found in the areas shown in dark green on this map. A few of the species may be very rare where you live. They may be common in other European countries, though, so you might have a chance to spot them if you go abroad.

Scandinavia

The British Isles

Mainland Europe

Keeping a record

There's an empty circle next to each picture. Whenever you spot a flower for the first time, you can put a tick in the circle.

Scorecard

At the end of the book is a scorecard. It gives an idea of how common each flower is. The most common species score 5 points and the rarest types score 25. If you want, you can add up your score after a day out spotting.

Species (name)	Score	Date spotted
Primula	5	
Red hot poker	20	14/07
Rhododendron	5	21/05
Rock cress	10	

You can fill in the scorecard like this.

5

Going spotting

What to take

Here are some useful things that you can take with you on a flower-spotting trip:

• This book to help you identify the flowers you see.

• Notepad and pencils so you can draw sketches of the things you find or jot down notes about them.

• A tape measure to help you measure the height of the plants or width of the flowers.

• A magnifying glass so you can take a closer look at the different parts of the flowers.

• A camera to take photographs of the flowers you've spotted.

These are the types of notes you can make to help you identify your finds.

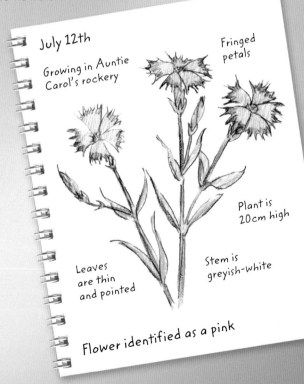

July 12th

Growing in Auntie Carol's rockery

Fringed petals

Plant is 20cm high

Stem is greyish-white

Leaves are thin and pointed

Flower identified as a pink

Photographing flowers

Making a photo album is a fun way to keep a record of the garden flowers you've seen. Here are a few tips on how to take a good picture of a flower:

Keep the Sun behind you and make sure your shadow doesn't fall across the flower as you're taking the photo.

If there isn't much light you may need to use the camera's flash.

If the flower is difficult to see amongst leaves or grass, place a piece of card behind it to make a plain background.

To pick or not to pick

Before you pick a flower from someone's garden, make sure you have permission from the owner. It's important never to pick or dig up flowers that are growing in the wild or in public places – look, but don't pick, so that others can enjoy them too.

You could use your camera's zoom function to take close-up pictures of the intricate parts of a flower that you wouldn't normally see, such as the wiry middle of this love-in-a-mist.

About garden flowers

Originally, all garden flowers were wild. Some, such as willow gentians, are native to Britain and Europe. Others were discovered further afield, for example African lilies, which were first found in South Africa. Plant hunters used to go on expeditions to difficult-to-reach and dangerous places to find exotic and colourful plants that could be grown in their gardens back home.

Rhododendrons, for instance, were brought to Britain in 1656 after an expedition to the Austrian Alps.

Rhododendrons are common in gardens all over Europe but are originally from mountain slopes.

After bringing the exotic flowers back, plant breeders used them to develop new varieties of the plants, that were stronger or of a different colour from the originals. If you go abroad on holiday, you might see garden plants growing wild in their native habitats.

As their name suggests, African lilies are originally from South Africa.

Where to look

A plant's home provides all the things it needs to survive. Most common garden flowers can grow almost anywhere. Others are more rare because they need certain conditions, such as constant warmth or plenty of rain, to grow well.

Crane's-bills are common garden flowers as they can grow in many different conditions.

You don't need to have a garden to spot garden plants. Once you start looking for flowers, you'll be surprised where you find them.

Here are some other places where you might find garden flowers:

- Window boxes and hanging baskets
- Florists' shops and supermarkets
- Garden centres and nurseries
- Flower tubs in shopping centres
- Flower beds outside public buildings
- Parks and zoos
- Public gardens and the grounds of stately homes
- Churchyards and cemeteries

You might see large beds of a single type of flower growing in parks, like this swathe of daffodils in London's St. James's Park.

Flowers, fruits and seeds

About flowers

A flower is a plant's seed-making factory. Seeds form when grains of pollen, made by a flower, are carried by insects, animals or the wind to another flower of the same type. The pollen then joins with cells called ovules inside the flower. These develop into seeds, which grow into new plants.

Pistil

Stigma

Ovary

Stamens

Pistil

Some pistils have a neck part, called a style, between the stigma and ovary.

The flower's male parts are called stamens. The blobby tip of the stamen is called the anther. This is where pollen is made.

Anther

Stamens

The flower's female part is called the pistil. The tip is the stigma, and the bottom part is the ovary, which contains the ovules.

The purpose of petals

The shape, colour, pattern and smell of petals can help to protect the flower's pollen, and attract and guide insects to its nectar – a sweet liquid that insects like to eat.

Purple nectar guides

Petals on drooping flowers shield the pollen from rainfall.

Flower arrangements

A plant might have one flower growing on a single stem, or many small flowers arranged in a bunch. Sometimes, what you might think is a single flower is actually made up of lots of smaller flowers, called florets.

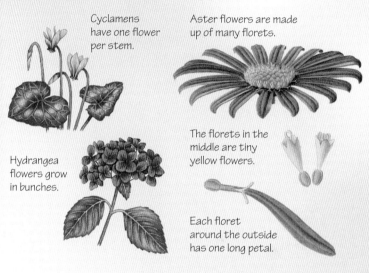

Cyclamens have one flower per stem.

Aster flowers are made up of many florets.

Hydrangea flowers grow in bunches.

The florets in the middle are tiny yellow flowers.

Each floret around the outside has one long petal.

About fruits and seeds

Once seeds begin to grow inside a flower, its petals fall off and the pistil swells, forming a fruit. Fruits can be fleshy and juicy or hard and dry.

Ornamental quince fruit is juicy and succulent.

Seeds

Sweet pea fruits are dry seed pods.

Looking at leaves

About leaves

Leaves are like little kitchens, making food for the plant. Using energy from sunlight, they combine raw ingredients of water and carbon dioxide gas to make a sugary substance that the plant needs to grow.

A leaf's veins carry water from the roots and take food to the rest of the plant.

The green colouring in a leaf traps energy from sunlight.

Holes that are too tiny to see, mainly in the underside of a leaf, let in carbon dioxide from the air.

Close-up of veins

Identifying leaves

If you find a plant whose flowers haven't opened yet, you might still be able to identify it by its leaves. Look out for the different ways in which leaves can be arranged on the stem of a plant.

A winter aconite's leaves grow in rings called whorls.

The leaves of a rose of Sharon grow in opposite pairs.

Bottle brush leaves grow alternately on each side of the stem.

Polyanthus leaves form a rosette at the base of its stem.

Parts and divisions

Leaves can be one shape, be made up of several parts, or have many tiny leaves, called leaflets, on one stalk.

Each of these nasturtium leaves is one large shape.

Each columbine leaf divides into three parts, joined at the base.

Rosa moyesii plants have little leaflets on a single stalk.

Shapes and edges

Leaves come in many shapes and sizes. Their outlines can be smooth, wavy or jagged.

Morning glories have smooth, heart-shaped leaves.

The edges of pelargonium leaves are wavy.

Toothed leaves are jagged, like the ones on this catmint.

A flowering currant's leaves are lobed, which means partially divided.

A Californian poppy's leaves are fine and feathery.

The leaves of globe thistles are edged with prickly spikes.

13

Blue flowers

➡ Californian lilac

Tall, evergreen, bushy shrub.
Shiny, oval, pointed leaves.
Tiny flowers in small clusters.
Attracts lots of insects.
Grows well against walls.
3m tall. Early summer.

Bunches of
many tiny
flowers

Buds

Close-up
of flower

Buds

⬅ Delphinium

Herbaceous plant with
deeply toothed leaves.
Long spike of flowers with
small, flowering side shoots.
Can also be mauve or
white. 1-1.5m tall. Summer.

➡ Grape hyacinth

Tiny flowers form triangular
spike. Strap-like leaves. Bell-
shaped flowers. Grows from
a bulb. 10-20cm tall. Spring.

Close-up
of flowers

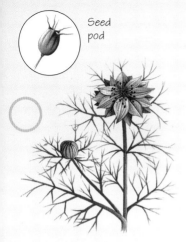

Seed pod

◀ Love-in-a-mist

Fern-like, delicate leaves on stems and under flowers. Flower looks like a cornflower. Can also be pink or white. Dried seed pods keep well. 40cm tall. Summer.

➡ African lily

Plant has many flowers in a rounded head. Many long, thick leaves at base, none on stems. Grows well in pots. Likes a sunny position. 60-90cm tall. Summer.

Stamens

Bare stem

Strap-shaped leaves

Buds are pink

Yellow eye

◀ Forget-me-not

Each small flower has a tiny yellow "eye". Leaves are covered in fine hairs. Flowers can also be white or pink. Often used as ground cover. 25cm tall. Spring.

15

➡ Willow gentian

Narrow leaves like a
willow. Long stems.
Trumpet-shaped flowers
with purple spots on inside.
30-60cm tall. Summer.

Sepals ——

⬅ Bell flower

Spreading plant with
bell-shaped flowers on
long stems. 25-50cm
tall. Summer.

➡ Globe thistle

Prickly leaves, prickly
rounded flowerheads.
Flowers dry well for winter
decorations. 1.2m tall.
Late summer.

Prickle
on leaf
tooth

← Periwinkle

Creeping plant. The trailing stems put down roots where they touch the soil, then grow flowering shoots. Likes shade. 1m long. Spring-summer.

— Shiny leaf

— Trailing stem

➡ Morning glory

A climbing plant with heart-shaped leaves. Large, trumpet-shaped flowers last a day. Open in the morning, close up at night. Up to 3m tall. Summer.

Lowest flowers open first

— Climbing stem

← Glory-of-the-snow

A stem of star-shaped flowers. Leaves blunt-tipped and strap-shaped. In borders and rock gardens. 5-10cm tall. Early spring.

Purple nectar guides

Woody stem

← Hibiscus

Branching, deciduous shrub. Three-lobed leaves with rounded, toothed margins. Large flowers, borne singly or in pairs, do not last long. 1.8-3m tall. Summer-autumn.

→ Scabious

Daisy-like flowers with central disc and pink anthers. Toothed, sword-shaped leaves. Dried seed pod is used in flower arrangements. 45-60cm tall. Summer-autumn.

Toothed leaves

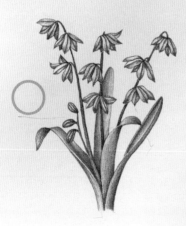

← Winter squill

Glossy, strap-shaped leaves appear first, followed by brilliant blue, bell-shaped flowers. Planted in rock gardens and borders. 15cm tall. Early spring.

◀ Lobelia

Small plant, usually seen in hanging baskets. Toothed, narrow leaves. Many small, delicate flowers, with white markings at the base of the petals. 10-25cm tall. Summer.

➡ Cornflower

Stiff, upright plant with narrow, pointed leaves that feel cottony. Often used for flower arrangements. 50-60cm tall. Summer.

Bud

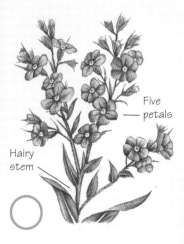

Five petals

Hairy stem

◀ Alkanet

Leaves are long and narrow. Small, round, flat flowers with white centres. Hairy stems and leaves. Could be confused with forget-me-not. Up to 1.5m tall. Summer.

➡ Rosemary

Narrow, strap-shaped leaves that feel downy on undersides, and smell when crushed. They are used in cooking. Insects land on the lips of the flowers. Up to 1.5m tall. Summer.

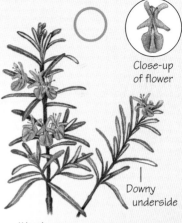

Close-up of flower

Downy underside

Woody stem

⬅ Catmint

Small, oval, toothed leaves, with a smell that attracts cats. Small, hooded flowers, arranged in whorls up the stem. Used in borders. 30-60cm tall. Summer-autumn.

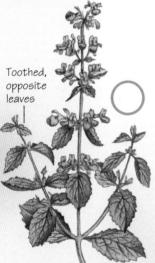

Toothed, opposite leaves

➡ Crane's-bill

Leaves deeply lobed and toothed. Flowers deeper purple towards the centre, with long styles. Seed pod looks like a bird's head and beak. 30-60cm tall. Mid-summer.

Young seed pod

Purple flowers

➡ Lilac

Large, upright shrub or small tree. Scented bunches of tiny flowers. Each flower has four petals. Leaves are heart- or egg-shaped. 2.5-3.5m tall. Late spring.

Bunches of many tiny flowers

Yellow disc attracts insects

Alternate leaves

⬅ Michaelmas daisy

Branching, upright plant. Has sprays of small, daisy-like flowers with yellow centres. Thin, pointed leaves. Good for cut flowers. 90cm tall. Autumn.

➡ Primula

Many small, primrose-like flowers, clustered together to form a dense head. Leaves form a rosette at the base of stem. Likes wet places. 30cm tall. Late spring.

Close-up of flower

Rosette of leaves

21

➤ Aubretia

Spreading plant, grows on walls or in rock gardens. Small flowers, with four rounded petals. Leaves are hairy and toothed. 5-10cm tall. Spring.

Close-up of flower

◀ Wisteria

Hanging, scented bunches of flowers. Oval, pointed leaflets often appear after the flowers. Climbing shrub, often grown up walls. Up to 10m high. Spring-summer.

Woody main stem

Flowers may appear before leaves

Close-up of flower

➤ Hosta

Trumpet-shaped flowers on a bare stem. Leaves, in a rosette around base of stem, are heart-shaped and heavily veined, with long stems. 60-90cm tall. Summer.

Large leaves

← Hebe

Evergreen, flowering shrub. Small tight bunches of tiny flowers, with four different-sized petals. Long style and stamens. Glossy leaves. Up to 1.2m tall. Summer-autumn.

Long stamens and styles

Shiny leaves

Flower head is made up of tiny flowers

→ Buddleja / buddleia / butterfly bush

Tall, shrubby plant which attracts butterflies. Long, upright, bunches of tiny, sweet-scented flowers. Long, pointed leaves. 3m tall. Summer-autumn.

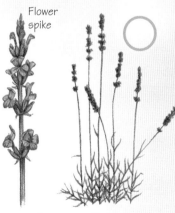

Flower spike

Leaves smell when rubbed

← Lavender

Spikes of flowers at end of long, square stems. Stems and leaves are downy. Long, thin leaves. Dried flowers are used to make scented bags. Up to 1.2m tall. Summer.

23

Pink flowers

➡ Pink magnolia

Large, woody shrub.
Goblet-shaped flowers
have petals that drop off
easily. They bloom on bare
branches. Leaves appear
later. 3-5m tall. Spring.

Petals drop
off easily —

Very young leaves

⬅ Rose campion

Flowers bloom for short time
only. May also be white.
Branching stems. Opposite
leaves are soft, woolly,
whitish and pointed. Up to
60cm tall. Mid-late summer.

Opposite
leaves

Pink
flower
stem ——

➡ Elephant's ears

Large clusters of small,
bell-shaped flowers on
a pink flower stem. Large,
oval, glossy leaves. Likes
shade. Used as ground
cover. 30cm tall. Spring.

Glossy leaves

➡ Weigela

Wide-spreading shrub
with arched branches.
Trumpet-shaped flowers
grow in clusters, and
bloom for a short time.
Oval, toothed leaves.
2m tall. Early summer.

Five petals
joined into
a tube

Five
petals

⬅ Pink

Fragrant, flat flowers.
Fringed petals. Greyish-
white stem and leaves.
Thin and pointed leaves.
Used in rock gardens.
12-30cm tall. Summer.

Style
longer
than
stamens

➡ Rhododendron

Large, evergreen shrub.
Flowerheads made up
of funnel-shaped flowers,
each 6-8cm across.
Large oval leaves. Can
be other colours. 3-4.5m
tall. Spring-summer.

Glossy
leaves

Stem curls up after flowering

Bud about to open

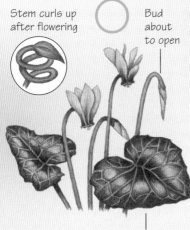

Shiny heart-shaped leaf

◀ Cyclamen

Flowers point downwards. The heart-shaped leaves have markings which differ from plant to plant. Prefers a shady position. 12-15cm tall. Autumn.

Early bud —

Mature bud

➡ Hollyhock

Tall spikes of flowers. May be different colours. The leaves are lobed, rough and hairy. Often in borders. Likes the sun. 1.2-1.5m tall. Summer.

Glossy evergreen leaves

◀ Camellia

Flowers richly coloured. Can be red, white or pink. Cup-shaped and 5-10cm across. Often spoiled by frosts. Glossy, dark leaves. Evergreen shrub. 1.8-2.5m tall. Winter-spring.

➡ Begonia

Large, glossy leaves, from green to dark purple. Many small flowers, each with two large and two smaller petals. A good pot plant. 15-25cm tall. Summer.

Glossy leaves

Flat flower bud

Long style

Bare stem

⬅ Belladonna lily

Strap-shaped leaves appear after the flowers. Three or four large, trumpet-shaped flowers at end of stem. Long style and stamens. 60cm tall. Spring-summer.

➡ Stonecrop

Thick, fleshy, oval leaves. Wide flowerheads made up of tiny flowers. Stem snaps easily. Usually grown in borders. 45cm tall. Late summer.

Close-up of single flower

Thick leaves

27

Red flowers

➡ Fuchsia

Drooping flowers. Sepals
curl upwards. Inner petals
form a bell and are
usually a different colour.
A bushy shrub often
in pots. 1-3m tall.
Summer-autumn.

Hanging
flower

Long style

⬅ Oriental poppy

Look for black marks
at base of large, waxy
petals. Styles and
stamens are easy to see.
Hairy leaves and stem.
Seed pod dries easily.
70cm tall. Early summer.

Hairy
bud

Hairy
stem

➡ Ornamental quince

Small, glossy, oval leaves.
Two to four bowl-shaped
flowers, in clusters.
Scented, yellow fruits.
Woody stem has hard
thorns. 1.8m tall.
Spring-summer.

Fruit

Thorn

Waxy
flower

➡ Escallonia

Clusters of flowers with red flower stems. Small, oval, toothed, glossy leaves. Can stand salt spray and sea gales. Hedging plant. 1.8m tall. Summer-autumn.

Flowers have red stems

Circle of flowers around stem

Red bracts

⬅ Bergamot

Bright red flowers attract bees and butterflies. Scented leaves can be dried and used in tea. Whorls of red bracts below whorls of red flowers. 60-90cm tall. Summer.

Flat flower

➡ Rosa moyesii

A tall shrub rose. Red flowers are followed by shiny red fruits that look like small bottles. Thin stems. Up to 2m tall. Mid-summer.

Red fruit, called a hip

29

← Sweet William

Scented, densely packed, single or double flowers. Pointed leaves. Used in borders. 30-60cm tall. Summer.

Close-up of single flower

Opposite leaves

→ Red hot poker

Tubular flowers with open ends pointing down, close together on poker-like spikes. Long, thin, pointed leaves. 90cm tall. Summer.

Red buds

New leaves growing at end of flower stem

Alternate leaves

← Bottle brush

Graceful, evergreen shrub. Flowers look like brushes used for cleaning bottles. New leaves grow from end of flower stem. 1.5-1.8m tall. Summer.

← Peony

Large, globe-shaped flowers. Can be other colours. Most leaves are lobed, some unlobed. Some leaves are hairy. Likes lots of sun and moisture. 60cm tall. Spring-summer.

Lobed leaf

Unlobed leaf

➡ Canna lily

Leaves vary in colour; are large, oval and thick-stemmed. Cluster of large, showy brightly coloured flowers on long stem. 1.5-2m tall. Summer.

Many tiny flowers

← Astilbe

The many tiny flowers form feathery spikes. Has dark green, toothed leaves. Likes shade and moisture. Can be other colours. 60-70cm tall. Mid-summer.

31

➡ Scarlet sage

Long, thin, hooded
flowers on a spike.
Red flower stem. Oval
leaves with toothed
edges. A summer
bedding plant.
30-90cm tall. Summer.

Close-up
of flower
on red stem

⬅ Love-lies-bleeding

Many small, drooping
flowers form a tassel, up
to 45cm long. Reddish,
drooping stems. Large oval
leaves, which can also be
red and yellow. 1.2m tall.
Mid-late summer.

Hanging
tassel of
many tiny
flowers

Fruit
or hip

➡ Japanese rose

Lots of small, thin prickles
on branches. Wrinkled
leaves. Single, scented
flowers. Round, orange-red
fruit appears in autumn.
2m tall. Summer-autumn.

Many thin prickles

➡ Fig marigold

Low, spreading plant. Narrow, light green leaves, with a sugary appearance. Daisy-like flowers open only in sunshine. Can be other bright colours. 15cm tall. Summer.

⬅ Pelargonium

Rounded, pale leaves with darker ring. Large head of flowers, which can also be other colours. Can be used as a pot plant. 50cm tall. Summer.

If you crush the leaf, it has a strong smell

Leaf has a strong smell

Deep veins in leaves

➡ Flowering currant

Drooping bunches of small, unpleasant-smelling flowers. Small deeply lobed leaves, which smell when crushed. Small autumn berries. 1.5-2m tall. Spring.

Orange flowers

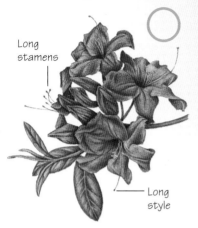

Long stamens

Long style

← Azalea

Bushy shrub. Flowers in clusters, often with a stong scent. Can also be red, yellow, pink or white. Oval leaves. 0.5-3m tall. Spring-summer.

Zigzag arrangement of flowers

➡ Montbretia

Delicate flowers grow in spikes. Long, thin, pointed leaves have raised ribs and grow from base. Spreads very easily. 60cm tall. Late summer.

← Pot marigold

Bushy annual with large daisy-like flowers. Long narrow leaves. Grown in borders and in pots for winter cutting. Petals may close at night. 30-40cm tall. Summer-autumn.

← Daylily

Herbaceous plants forming large clumps. Flowers have long style and stamens; last one day. Arching, strap-like leaves. 0.6-1.0m tall. Mid-summer.

→ Crown imperial

Narrow, glossy leaves. Bell-shaped flowers hang in clusters under leaves. Have long stamens hanging below petals. Brown stem. 60-90cm tall. Spring.

Flowers under leaves

Long stamens

Spur

← Nasturtium

Faintly scented, trumpet-shaped flowers. Leaves have wavy edges and smell like cabbages. Climbing or creeping plants. 20-40cm tall; taller if growing up a support. Summer-autumn.

35

➡ Orange ball tree

An upright, evergreen shrub, with long, thin, wrinkled leaves. Small, scented flowers in tight, round heads. Opposite leaves. 5m tall. Summer.

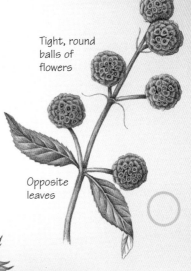

Tight, round balls of flowers

Opposite leaves

Toothed lobes

⬅ Globe flower

Globe-shaped flowers like huge buttercups. Leaves with toothed divisions. Used for borders or sides of ponds. 60cm tall. Summer.

➡ Peruvian lily

Long-lasting, trumpet-shaped flowers, borne on thin, leafy stalks. Upper two petals have red-brown markings. Long stem. 90cm tall. Summer.

36

➡ French marigold

Yellow-orange flowers with dark centres. Toothed, feathery leaves. Strong smell when leaves are rubbed. Good for borders. 15-30cm tall. Summer.

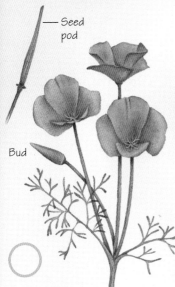

— Seed pod

Bud

⬅ Californian poppy

Finely cut leaves. Delicate, saucer-shaped flowers that close in dull weather. Cone-shaped buds, and long seed pods. 30-45cm tall. Summer.

Bud

➡ Avens

Long-lasting, saucer-shaped flowers, can be double. Deeply toothed leaves. A border plant which is very easy to grow. 30cm tall. Spring-summer.

Deeply toothed leaves

White flowers

◀ Bull bay

Large, evergreen shrub, with bowl-shaped, scented flowers. Rhododendron-like glossy leaves with orange undersides. Soft, downy, sepals around bud. 3-10m tall. Summer.

➡ Evergreen candytuft

Grows in thick, flat clusters. Good for town gardens because it blooms in smoke and dirt. 10-20cm tall. Early summer.

Inner petals tinged with green

◀ Snowdrop

Drooping flowers with three, short inner petals and three, longer outer petals. Flat, long, strap-shaped leaves. 8-20cm tall. Winter-spring.

➡ Shasta daisy

Herbaceous plant. Has large, daisy-like flowers with yellow centres. Big, smooth, toothed leaves. Look for cut flowers in florists' shops. 50-150cm tall. Summer.

Bud

⬅ Deutzia

Flowers in clusters. Bushy plant has branches growing straight up, with peeling bark. 1.8-3m tall. Mid-summer.

Opposite leaves

➡ Pampas grass

Silky, flowering plumes, 30-45cm long. Thick mass of slender, arching, sharp-edged leaves. Likes a sunny position. Often in parks. 1.5-3m tall. Summer-autumn.

➡ Mock orange

Large, woody shrub with small, cup-shaped flowers. Oval, veined leaves. Flowers smell like orange blossom. Petals drop easily. Likes part-shade. 1.5-3m tall. Summer.

Bud

⬅ Japanese anemone

Flowers in groups on long branching stems. Can also be pink. Leaves at base of stems are deeply lobed. 1.2-1.5m tall. Late summer.

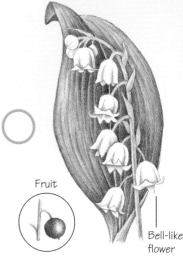

➡ Lily-of-the-valley

Arching stems with five to eight sweet-smelling, bell-shaped, waxy flowers. Pairs of broad leaves have parallel veins. Red fruits. 20cm tall. Spring.

Fruit

Bell-like flower

➡ Mexican orange

Sweet-smelling flowers grow
in clusters. Glossy leaves
smell when they are
crushed. 1.5-2m tall.
Early summer.

Close-up
of flower

⬅ Baby's breath

Bushy, dome-shaped
plant. Many tiny, star-
shaped flowers. Thin,
pointed, opposite leaves.
1m tall. Summer.

Opposite
leaves

➡ Christmas rose

Plant has saucer-
shaped flowers and
dark, tough, evergreen
leaves. Likes part-shade
where it is protected
from winter frosts.
30cm tall. Winter.

← Rock cress

Small, evergreen plant, grown on walls and banks. Long, rounded leaves. Small flowers with four petals. Sweetly scented. Easy to grow. 20cm tall. Spring-summer.

Pink buds

Glossy leaves

➡ Laurustinus

Bushy evergreen shrub with pointed oval leaves. Small flowers are in a flat head, 6-8cm across. Sweet smell. 2-3m tall. Winter-spring.

Yellow stigma

Orange anthers

← Madonna lily

Tall upright plant with long, strap-shaped leaves. Hanging flowers, 5-8cm long, borne singly on the stem. Bright orange anthers. Sweet scented. 1.5m tall. Summer.

Yellow

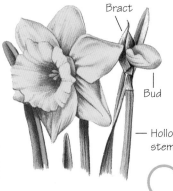

Bract

Bud

Hollow stem

← Daffodil

Flower has six, flat petals, and trumpet-shaped cup. Strap-shaped leaves. 15-60cm tall. Spring.

→ Wallflower

Upright, bushy plant. Sweet-smelling flowers can also be pink, reddish orange and off-white. Likes a sunny position. In borders. 30-60cm tall. Late spring.

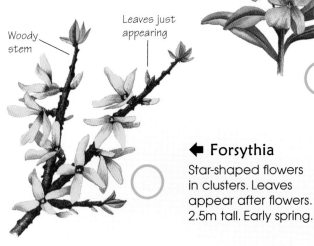

Woody stem

Leaves just appearing

← Forsythia

Star-shaped flowers in clusters. Leaves appear after flowers. 2.5m tall. Early spring.

➡ Rock rose

Small, spreading shrub, with saucer-shaped flowers which have papery petals. Opposite, hairy leaves. In rock gardens and borders. 25cm tall. Summer.

Seeds ripen in centre of flower

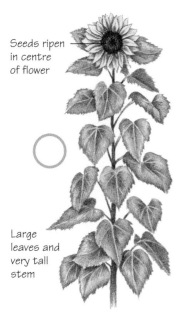

Large leaves and very tall stem

⬅ Sunflower

Heart-shaped, toothed leaves and hairy stems. Flowers are 35cm across. Seeds can be dried for bird food. 1.5-3m tall. Summer.

Close-up of flower

➡ Gold dust

Small bedding plant with tiny, strap-shaped, hairy leaves and quite large clusters of sweet-smelling flowers. In borders. 20cm tall. All summer.

➡ Winter aconite

One cup-shaped flower on a stem, with a circle of deeply cut, pale leaves under it. Seeds spread easily. In borders and under trees. 10cm tall. Early spring.

Whorl of leaves around flower

Bare stems

Masses of tiny flowers

⬅ Goldenrod

Tiny, feathery flowers form clusters. Long leaves, rough on top, at alternate points up stem. In sunny borders. Up to 1.8m tall. Summer-autumn.

➡ Brachyglottis 'Sunshine'

Daisy-like flowers grow in clusters. Thick, oval-shaped leaves have greyish-white felt on undersides. Can be quite bushy. Up to 1.5m tall. Summer.

White underside of leaf

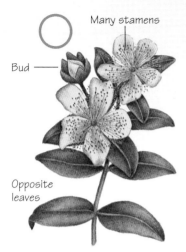

Many stamens

Bud

Opposite leaves

← Rose of Sharon

A low shrub, keeps leaves all year. Flowers have five petals and many long stamens. Leaves have waxy coating. 1m tall. Summer.

Spotted sepals

→ Evening primrose

Funnel-shaped flowers are scented, opening in the evening. Leaves are long, deeply veined with marks underneath. 1.5m tall. Summer.

Leaves have prickly edges

← Oregon grape

Evergreen shrub with glossy, prickly-edged leaves. Scented, tiny flowers in bunches. Grape-like berries appear later. Up to 1.5m tall. Spring.

← Broom

Upright shrub with tiny leaves and green stems. Many small flowers, single or in pairs. Sweet scented. Seed pods explode in hot weather. 2.5m tall. Early summer.

Seed

Seed pod

→ Coneflower

Petals point down. Raised, greenish, cone-shaped centres. Leaves are oval, pointed, deeply toothed. 1m tall. Late summer.

Central cone

Flowerhead made up of many tiny flowers

← Milfoil

Delicate, deeply cut, feathery leaves. Tiny flowers borne in large flat heads, 10-15cm across. Easy to grow in borders. 60cm tall. Late summer.

➡ Potentilla fructicosa

Look in borders and car parks. Saucer-shaped flowers have five petals. A shrub, with tough stems and many branches. Likes a sunny position. 1m tall. Spring-autumn.

Five petals

Bud

⬅ Leopard's bane

Daisy-like flowers on long stalks. Toothed, heart-shaped leaves. In borders, but prefers semi-shade. Good for cut flowers. 60cm tall. Spring-summer.

➡ Honeysuckle

Long, tube-shaped, scented flowers growing in clusters. Only lower leaves are on stalks. Poisonous fruit in autumn. A climber. 2.3m tall; taller if growing up a support. Summer.

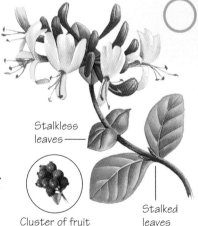

Stalkless leaves

Stalked leaves

Cluster of fruit

48

➡ Winter jasmine

Deep green stem

Flowers appear before the leaves. Small, trumpet-shaped flowers. Tough, deep green stem. Small glossy leaves. Can be trained to grow up walls. Up to 3m tall. Winter.

⬅ Sneezeweed

Long, thin, toothed leaves. Flowers with wavy-edged petals and large central discs. Look in sunny borders. Makes good cut flowers. 1-1.5m tall. Summer-autumn.

➡ Tickseed

The petals have ragged edges. Long thin leaves and round buds. Spreads easily and makes good cut flowers. Look in borders. 45-90cm tall. Summer.

Flowers that can be various colours

Close-up of flower

Yellow eye

◀ Polyanthus

Clusters of primrose-like flowers on stout stems, with rosette of leaves at base. Can be a variety of colours. Suitable for window-boxes. 15cm tall. Summer.

Spike of flowers

➡ Lupin

A spike of small flowers 60cm tall. Leaf made up of 5-15 small leaflets. Spreads easily. Found in borders. Up to 1.5m tall. Summer.

◀ China aster

Large, round flower, with lots of petals. Hairy, deeply lobed leaves. Look in sunny borders. Good cut flowers. 20-60cm tall. Summer.

← Hyacinth

Many small, waxy, sweet-smelling flowers on one or two thick stems. Long, thin leaves grow from the base of the plant. Can be grown in pots. 30-50cm tall. Early spring.

Close-up of flower

➡ Clematis

A climbing plant, used on walls or fences. The flower can be purple, blue, pink, white or yellow. 1.5-3m tall. Summer.

Heart-shaped leaf

← Zinnia

Brightly coloured, daisy-like flowers. Opposite leaves are oval and pointed. Used as a summer bedding plant. Good cut flowers. 60-75cm tall. Summer.

51

➡ Pansy

Flowers have five petals with a velvet-like feel. Can be many colours, usually with a dark centre. Common summer bedding plant. 15-22cm tall. Spring-summer.

⬅ Dahlia

Flower single or double with a ring of petals round a central disc. Look in florists' shops. In borders. 1m tall. Late summer.

Bud

Other kinds of dahlia have lighter green leaves.

Coloured veins on petals

➡ Crocus

Flower grows straight from ground; has six oval-shaped petals. Thin, short, pointed leaves with a central white stripe. Often in parks. 10-20cm tall. Early spring.

White stripe down centre of leaf

Papery bract

➡ Hybrid tea rose

The familiar rose. Sweet-smelling flowers with cone-shaped buds. Prickly stems and glossy leaves in groups. Amber fruits in autumn. Up to 1.2m tall. All summer.

Close-up of flower

Petals are joined to form a tube —

⬅ Foxglove

Spotted, bell-shaped flowers on one side only of tall spike. Leaves grow from base of spike. Up to 1.5m tall. Summer-autumn.

➡ Phlox

Sweet smelling, flat flowers grow in clusters. Long, thin leaves. Often used in borders. Good for cut flowers. Up to 1m tall. Summer-autumn.

53

← Beard tongue

Snapdragon-like, open-mouthed, drooping flowers. Small, thin, pointed leaves. This is a short-lived bedding plant. 60cm tall. Summer.

Opposite leaves

→ Iris

The lower, drooping petals have hairs called beards. The leaves are sword-like. Up to 1.2m tall. Early summer.

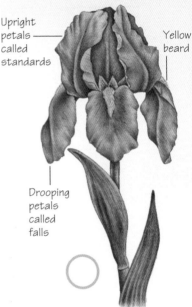

Upright petals called standards

Yellow beard

Drooping petals called falls

Waxy petals

Stem snaps easily

← Tulip

Popular garden flower with waxy, heavy petals that open in sunlight. A few broad leaves and an unbranched stem. 70cm tall. Spring.

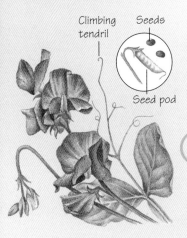

Climbing tendril

Seeds

Seed pod

← Sweet pea

Flowers highly scented. Can be many colours. Leaves in pairs. Plant has tendrils. Up to 2.5m tall. Summer.

Seed pod

Remains of style

➡ Snapdragon

Flowers grow in spikes, and are tube-shaped with a hinged, spreading lip. Look in borders. Up to 60cm tall. Spring-autumn.

← Hydrangea

Showy balls of flowers on a large, bushy shrub. Flowerheads can be dried and used for decorations. Up to 2m tall. Summer.

Toothed leaf

55

➡ Petunia

Common in hanging baskets.
A low-growing or trailing
plant with large, trumpet-
shaped, open flowers.
Leaves are pointed and
oval. Used in window
boxes. 30-45cm tall.
Summer.

—Bud

⬅ Gladiolus

The flowers all face the same
way on thick stems, and
grow to form a spike. Sword-
shaped leaves. In borders.
Also look in florists' shops.
50-100cm tall. Mid-summer.

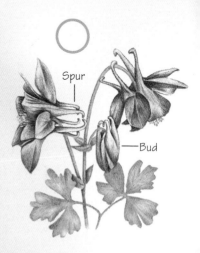

Spur

—Bud

➡ Columbine

Nodding, delicate
flowers. Look for long,
showy spurs on petals.
Branching stems with a
single flower on each one.
Up to 1m tall. Late spring.

Botanical names

As well as their common names, flowers also have botanical names, which are used by flower experts around the world. Here are the botanical names for all the flowers in this book.

Blue flowers

p.14   Ceanothus x veitchianus
        Delphinium cultivar
        Muscari armeniacum
p.15   Nigella damascena
        Agapanthus campanulatus
        Myosotis alpestris
p.16   Gentiana asclepiadea
        Campanula carpatica
        Echinops ritro
p.17   Vinca minor
        Ipomoea tricolor
        Chionodoxa luciliae
p.18   Hibiscus syriacus
        Scabiosa caucasica
        Scilla siberica
p.19   Lobelia erinus
        Centaurea cyanus
        Anchusa azurea
p.20   Rosmarinus officinalis
        Nepeta faassenii
        Geranium ibericum

Purple flowers

p.21   Syringa vulgaris
        Aster novi-belgii
        Primula denticulata
p.22   Aubrieta deltoidea
        Wisteria sinensis
        Hosta fortunei
p.23   Hebe 'Autumn Glory'
        Buddleja davidii
        Lavandula angustifolia

Pink flowers

p.24   Magnolia x soulangeana
        Lychnis coronaria
        Bergenia cordifolia
p.25   Weigela 'Abel Carrière'
        Dianthus plumarius
        Rhododendron 'Pink Pearl'
p.26   Cyclamen hederifolium
        Althaea rosea
        Camellia x williamsii
p.27   Begonia semperflorens
        Amaryllis belladonna
        Sedum spectabile

Red flowers

p.28   Fuchsia magellanica
        Papaver orientale
        Chaenomeles speciosa 'Simonii'
p.29   Escallonia cultivar
        Monarda didyma
        Rosa moyesii
p.30   Dianthus barbatus
        Kniphofia cultivar
        Callistemon citrinus
p.31   Paeonia officinalis cultivar
        Canna x ehemanii
        Astilbe x arendsii
p.32   Salvia splendens
        Amaranthus caudatus
        Rosa rugosa
p.33   Dorotheanus bellidiformis
        Pelargonium Zonal cultivar
        Ribes sanguineum

Orange flowers

White flowers

Yellow flowers

Various colours

Useful words

This page explains some words you might come across when reading about flowers. Words that are written in *italic text* are defined separately.

annual – a plant that lives only for one year

bedding plant – a low-growing *annual* plant, used in flowerbeds to cover the ground

border – a strip of ground in a garden, often used specifically for growing flowers

bract – a leaf-like part of a plant at the base of a flower or stalk

bud – an undeveloped *shoot*, leaf or flower

bulb – a thick, underground *bud* which a plant uses to store food and produce new plants

bush – another word for *shrub*

climbing plant – a plant that grows upwards using a fence, a wall, or another plant for support

creeping plant – a plant that grows along the ground

deciduous – a tree or *shrub* that loses its leaves every year at the end of the growing season

double flower – a flower that has many overlapping petals, making it seem very full

downy – covered with fine, soft hairs

evergreen – a tree or *shrub* that is covered with leaves all year

flowerhead – a cluster of small flowers that often looks like a single flower

hedge – a row of closely planted *shrubs*

herbaceous – a plant with a fleshy, not woody, stem

hood – the curved, topmost petal of some flowers

lip – the hanging, lowermost petal of some flowers

native – originally from

nectar guides – patterns on some petals that guide insects to the nectar inside

rock garden – a garden that features lots of rocks and stones

seed pod – a tough, dry fruit

sepal – leaf-like parts of a plant that protect a flower while it is a *bud*

shoot – a young stem or leaf

shrub – a woody plant, smaller than a tree, with many branches growing from near the base

spike – a long *flowerhead* attached to a central stem

spur – a narrow, hollow cone at the base of a petal that sticks out behind a flower

tendril – a slender leaf or stem, which twines around objects for support

Scorecard

When you start spotting, you'll soon find that some flowers are rarer than others. To give you a rough idea of how likely you are to see them, all the flowers in the book are listed here with a score next to each one.

Species	Score	Date spotted	Species	Score	Date spotted
African lily	20		Camellia	15	
Alkanet	15		Canna lily	20	
Astilbe	20		Catmint	15	
Aubretia	10		China aster	10	
Avens	5		Christmas rose	20	
Azalea	5		Clematis	10	
Baby's breath	15		Columbine	10	
Beard tongue	15		Coneflower	15	
Begonia	10		Cornflower	10	
Bell flower	15		Crane's-bill	15	
Belladonna lily	25		Crocus	5	
Bergamot	20		Crown imperial	25	
Bottle brush	25		Cyclamen	20	
Brachyglottis 'Sunshine'	10		Dahlia	5	
Broom	5		Daffodil	5	
Buddleja / buddleia / butterfly bush	5		Daylily	20	
Bull bay	15		Delphinium	10	
Californian lilac	15		Deutzia	15	
Californian poppy	10		Elephant's ears	20	

Species	Score	Date spotted	Species	Score	Date spotted
Escallonia	15		Hybrid tea rose	5	
Evening primrose	15		Hydrangea	5	
Evergreen candytuft	5		Iris	10	
Fig marigold	25		Japanese anemone	15	
Flowering currant	10		Japanese rose	5	
Forget-me-not	5		Laurustinus	15	
Forsythia	5		Lavender	5	
Foxglove	5		Leopard's bane	10	
French marigold	5		Lilac	10	
Fuchsia	5		Lily-of-the-valley	10	
Gladiolus	10		Lobelia	5	
Globe flower	15		Love-in-a-mist	15	
Globe thistle	20		Love-lies-bleeding	20	
Glory-of-the-snow	10		Lupin	5	
Gold dust	15		Madonna lily	20	
Goldenrod	10		Mexican orange	20	
Grape hyacinth	10		Michaelmas daisy	5	
Hebe	10		Milfoil	10	
Hibiscus	20		Mock orange	10	
Hollyhock	10		Montbretia	15	
Honeysuckle	5		Morning glory	10	
Hosta	15		Nasturtium	5	
Hyacinth	5		Orange ball tree	20	

Species	Score	Date spotted	Species	Score	Date spotted
Oregon grape	10		Rose of Sharon	5	
Oriental poppy	15		Rosemary	10	
Ornamental quince	20		Scabious	15	
Pampas grass	15		Scarlet sage	5	
Pansy	5		Shasta daisy	10	
Pelargonium	10		Snapdragon	5	
Peony	10		Sneezeweed	20	
Periwinkle	10		Snowdrop	5	
Peruvian lily	20		Stonecrop	15	
Petunia	5		Sunflower	5	
Phlox	15		Sweet pea	5	
Pink	10		Sweet William	10	
Pink magnolia	10		Tickseed	15	
Polyanthus	5		Tulip	5	
Pot marigold	10		Wallflower	5	
Potentilla fructicosa	5		Weigela	10	
Primula	5		Willow gentian	25	
Red hot poker	20		Winter aconite	20	
Rhododendron	5		Winter jasmine	5	
Rock cress	10		Winter squill	15	
Rock rose	15		Wisteria	10	
Rosa moyesii	15		Zinnia	10	
Rose campion	20				

Index

Edited by Sarah Khan
Designed by Stephanie Jones and Joanne Kirkby
Digital manipulation by Keith Furnival

PHOTO CREDITS: Cover © J. Lilly / Garden World Images; 1 © Babette French / Alamy; 2-3 © Colin Underhill / Alamy; 7 © PNRF / Alamy; 8-9 © Alex Segre / Alamy

This edition first published in 2009 by Usborne Publishing Ltd, 83-85 Saffron Hill, London EC1N 8RT, England. www.usborne.com. Copyright © 2009, 1978 Usborne Publishing Ltd. The name Usborne and the devices ♀ ♛ are Trade Marks of Usborne Publishing Ltd.